tage 2
lore Patterned Stories A
ucy Tritton



# Group/Guided Reading Notes

## Contents

# Introduction

Oxford Reading Tree stories at Stages 1–4 feature settings and situations most children will find familiar. The stories reflect the experiences of most 4–6-year-olds: having a bath, going to a party, having new shoes, getting into trouble. Children of this age will readily identify with the characters and situations. This also helps build comprehension.

Each book tells a complete story, using natural language, phonically decodable words and high frequency words, all supported by funny and engaging pictures. The strongly patterned language helps children build up their sight vocabulary. The books also offer plenty of scope for developing children's word recognition and language comprehension skills. All this helps build children's confidence in their ability to read independently. When used alongside your systematic phonic teaching they will help children put all their reading skills into practice in a highly motivating way.

## Using the books

This booklet provides suggestions for using the books for guided, group and independent activities. The reading activities include ideas for developing children's *word recognition* W and *language comprehension* C skills. Within word recognition, there are ideas for helping children practise their phonic skills and knowledge, as well as helping them to tackle words that are not easy to decode phonically. The language comprehension ideas include suggestions for teaching the skills of prediction, questioning, clarifying, summarising and imagining in order to help children understand the text and the whole stories. Suggestions are also provided for speaking, listening, drama and writing activities.

## Reading fluency

To support children in developing fluency in their reading and give them plenty of opportunities to revisit the stories. This includes:

- rereading independently
- rereading with a partner
- rereading at home
- listening to audio versions of the story (e.g. Talking Stories)
- hearing the story read to them by others as they follow the printed text.

Rereading and rehearing helps children develop automatic word recognition and gives them models of fluent, expressive reading.

# Comprehension strategies

| Story | Comprehension strategies taught through these Group/Guided Reading Notes | | | | |
|---|---|---|---|---|---|
| | Prediction | Questioning | Clarifying | Summarising | Imagining |
| What Is It? | ✓ | ✓ | ✓ | ✓ | ✓ |
| The Lost Puppy | ✓ | ✓ | ✓ | ✓ | ✓ |
| New Trees | ✓ | | ✓ | ✓ | |
| Up and Down | ✓ | ✓ | ✓ | ✓ | |
| The Little Dragon | ✓ | ✓ | ✓ | ✓ | ✓ |
| The Band | ✓ | ✓ | ✓ | ✓ | |

# Vocabulary and phonic opportunities

The chart shows the main words used in each book. The decodable words listed should be decodable for most children at this Stage. The tricky words are very common but do not conform to the phonic rules taught up to this point – children will need support to learn and recognise them. If children struggle with one of these words you can model how to read it.

| | | |
|---|---|---|
| **What Is It?** | Decodable words | a, and, at, Biff, children, Chip, Floppy, frog, is, it, lizard, lost, Mum, safe, salamander, Wilf, Wilma |
| | Tricky words | barked, he, look(ed), said, she, was, what |
| **The Lost Puppy** | Decodable words | a, and, Biff, Chip, Dad, clever, dog, for, had, his, it, lost, May, Mum, off, puppy, ran, Sniff, tree, upset, Wilf, Wilma |
| | Tricky words | bone, called, could, couldn't, everyone, find, look(ed), Mrs, nobody, said, swing, the, they, was, what |
| **New Trees** | Decodable words | Biff, bridge, children, Chip, Dad, Floppy, funny, gave, in, it, pond, put, shed, to, week, went, Wilf, Wilma |
| | Tricky words | bone, everyone, give, he, hole, park, said, she, stream, the, wanted, was |
| **Up and Down** | Decodable words | a, and, book, came, Dad, down, Mum, see, shopping, stop, up, went |
| | Tricky words | couldn't, he, paintbrush, said, she, wanted |
| **The Little Dragon** | Decodable words | a, am, Biff, but, children, Chip, cross, dragon, in, king, Kipper, on, play, pond, pushed, put, tree, under, went |
| | Tricky words | everyone, fight, frightened, good, I, knight, like, little, princess, said, the, to, what, will, Wilma, with |
| **The Band** | Decodable words | a, at, bad, band, Dad, dog, Floppy, his, house, in, play(ed), shed, trumpet, went |
| | Tricky words | barked, couldn't, garage, he, park, said, the, to, what |

# Curriculum coverage chart

| | Speaking, listening, drama | Reading | Writing |
|---|---|---|---|
| **What Is It?** | | | |
| **PNS Literacy Framework** (YF) | 1.1, 3.2 | W 5.3<br>C 7.1, 7.3, 7.4 | 9.1 |
| **National Curriculum** | Working towards Level 1 | | |
| **Scotland (5–14)** (P1) | Level A | Level A | Level A |
| **N. Ireland** (P1/Y1) | Attention and listening 5<br>Language and thinking 4, 5, 11 | 1, 3, 4, 6, 8, 13, 17, 19, 21 | 1, 3, 4, 6, 11, 16 |
| **Wales** (Key Stage 1) | Range 1,3<br>Skills 2, 5, 6 | Range 2, 4, 6<br>Skills 1, 2<br>Language and development 1 | Range 1, 4<br>Skills 2, 3, 6, 8, 9 |
| **The Lost Puppy** | | | |
| **PNS Literacy Framework** (YF) | 1.1, 3.2, 4.1 | W 5.5<br>C 7.1, 7.4 | 9.1 |
| **National Curriculum** | Working towards Level 1 | | |
| **Scotland (5–14)** (P1) | Level A | Level A | Level A |
| **N. Ireland** (P1/Y1) | Attention and listening 5<br>Social use of language 3, 6<br>Language and thinking 1, 4, 7, 8, 9, 10, 11 | 1, 3, 4, 6, 8, 13, 17, 19, 21 | 1, 3, 4, 6, 10, 13, 14, 16 |
| **Wales** (Key Stage 1) | Range 1,3<br>Skills 2, 3, 4, 5, 6 | Range 2, 4, 6<br>Skills 1, 2<br>Language and development 1 | Range 1, 4, 6<br>Skills 2, 3, 7, 8, 9 |

**Key**

C = Language comprehension

W = Word recognition

Y = Year

F = Foundation/reception

P = Primary

In the designations such as 5.2, the first number represents the strand and the second number the bullet point

# Curriculum coverage chart

| | Speaking, listening, drama | Reading | Writing |
|---|---|---|---|
| **New Trees** | | | |
| **PNS Literacy Framework** (YF) | 1.4 | W 5.1<br>C 7.1, 7.2 | 11.1 |
| **National Curriculum** | Working towards Level 1 | | |
| **Scotland (5–14)** (P1) | Level A | Level A | Level A |
| **N. Ireland** (P1/Y1) | Social use of language 3<br>Language and thinking 5, 8, 9, 11<br>Extended vocabulary 3 | 1, 3, 4, 6, 8, 13, 17, 19, 21 | 1, 3, 4, 16 |
| **Wales** (Key Stage 1) | Range 1, 3<br>Skills 2, 3<br>Language and development 1, 2 | Range 2, 4, 6<br>Skills 1, 2<br>Language and development 1 | Range 1, 2<br>Skills 2, 3, 5, 6, 8, 9 |
| **Up and Down** | | | |
| **PNS Literacy Framework** (YF) | 3.2, 4.1 | W 5.9<br>C 7.1, 7.3 | 9.1 |
| **National Curriculum** | Working towards Level 1 | | |
| **Scotland (5–14)** (P1) | Level A | Level A | Level A |
| **N. Ireland** (P1/Y1) | Social use of language 5<br>Language and thinking 5, 6, 11 | 1, 3, 4, 6, 8, 13, 17, 19, 21 | 1, 3, 4, 16 |
| **Wales** (Key Stage 1) | Range 1, 2, 5<br>Skills 2, 5 | Range 2, 4, 6<br>Skills 1, 2<br>Language and development 1 | Range 1, 2, 4, 6<br>Skills 2, 3, 5, 6, 8, 9 |

# Curriculum coverage chart

| | Speaking, listening, drama | Reading | Writing |
|---|---|---|---|
| **The Little Dragon** | | | |
| **PNS Literacy Framework** (YF) | 1.1, 4.1 | W 5.10, 6.1<br>C 7.1, 8.3 | 9.1 |
| **National Curriculum** | Working towards Level 1 | | |
| **Scotland (5–14)** (P1) | Level A | Level A | Level A |
| **N. Ireland** (P1/Y1) | Social use of language 5, 6<br>Language and thinking 4, 5, 11 | 1, 3, 4, 6, 8, 13, 17, 19, 21 | 1, 3, 4, 6, 10, 11, 13, 16 |
| **Wales** (Key Stage 1) | Range 1, 3, 5<br>Skills 2, 5 | Range 2, 4, 6<br>Skills 1, 2<br>Language and development 1 | Range 1, 2, 4<br>Skills 2, 3, 5, 6, 8, 9 |
| **The Band** | | | |
| **PNS Literacy Framework** (YF) | 2.2, 3.2 | W 5.1<br>C 7.1, 7.3 | 11.1 |
| **National Curriculum** | Working towards Level 1 | | |
| **Scotland (5–14)** (P1) | Level A | Level A | Level A |
| **N. Ireland** (P1/Y1) | Attention and listening 2<br>Social use of language 3<br>Language and thinking 8, 11 | 1, 3, 4, 6, 8, 13, 17, 19, 21 | 1, 3, 4, 16 |
| **Wales** (Key Stage 1) | Range 1, 3<br>Skills 2, 4, 5, 6 | Range 2, 4, 6<br>Skills 1, 2<br>Language and development 1 | Range 1, 4<br>Skills 2, 3, 8, 9 |

# What Is It?

| | |
|---|---|
| **C** = Language comprehension | *R, AF* = QCA reading assessment focus |
| **W** = Word recognition | *W, AF* = QCA writing assessment focus |

## Group or guided reading

### Introducing the book

**C** *(Prediction)* Look at the cover and read the title. Ask the children: *What do you think it is?*

**C** *(Clarifying)* Look through the book at the illustrations, page by page, and talk about what is happening.

**W** Point out and read the words 'lizard' on page 11 and 'salamander' on page 14.

**C** *(Clarifying)* Ask: *What do you think the creature on the front cover is now?*

### Strategy check

Remind the children to read from left to right.

### Independent reading

- Ask children to read the story. Praise and encourage them while they read, and prompt as necessary.

**W** Praise the children for reading the high frequency words and CVC words on sight.

**W** Do children remember the words 'lizard' and 'salamander'? If not, remind them to sound out each letter to help read the word.

**Assessment** Check that children:

- *(R, AF1)* can read the high frequency words with confidence
- *(R, AF4)* track the text from left to right, top to bottom.

## Returning to the text

- C *(Summarising)* Ask the children to retell the story in one or two sentences.
- C *(Imagining)* Say: *Tell me how you think the salamander ended up in the park.*
- C *(Prediction, Questioning)* On page 16, ask: *What do you think will happen to the salamander now? Do you think the family did the right thing to take it to the animal rescue centre?*
  - On page 3, ask: *Who is saying 'What is it?' Tell me how she might have said this.* Talk about the 'question mark' sign and encourage children to say the words with the correct expression.
- W Ask the children to tell you what noise Floppy made at the start of the story. Ask: *Can you think of any other words that rhyme with 'bark'?* Encourage children to think of words, e.g. 'park', 'dark', 'ark'.
- C *(Clarifying)* Ask: *Why did Mum take a while to get to the children?*

# Group and independent reading activities

**Objective** Use talk to organise, sequence and clarify thinking (3.2). Show an understanding of the elements of stories, such as main character, sequence of events (7.3). Retell narratives in the correct sequence (7.4).

- C *(Summarising)* Ask: *What happened in the story first? Then what happened? What happened next? What happened at the end?*
  - Write down the children's suggestions on the board. Then all check in the book to see that the order of events is correct, e.g. Floppy barks; children find the creature; Mum says it is a salamander; they take it to the animal rescue centre.
  - Divide the class/group up into three. Say that one group is to be Floppy, the other the children and the final one, Mum (more able children).

- Ask each group to discuss what they say in the story, e.g. Floppy barks, children say 'What is it?', Mum says 'It's a salamander. It's lost.' Encourage the final group to add something about taking the salamander to the animal rescue centre, e.g. 'Let's take it to the animal rescue centre.'
- Ask each group to say their words in the correct sequence for a whole class/group performance.

**Assessment** *(R, AF2)* Are children able to retrieve information from the text? Do they speak clearly?

**Objective** Know that print carries meaning and, in English, is read from left to right (7.1).

**C** *(Clarifying)* Write the following sentences on card:

Mum looked at it.
"It's lost," she said.
Floppy barked and barked.

- Cut the cards in half so there are a couple of words on each side.
- Ask the children to find the two halves that make a sensible sentence.
- Children write down the whole sentence.

**Assessment** *(W, AF2)* Do children reread the sentences to check for sense?

**Objective** Recognise letter shapes and say a sound for each (5.3).

**W** Give the children letter cards.

- Ask them to find the letters to spell 'frog' on page 9 of the book.
- When they find each letter ask them to tell you its letter sounds.
- Repeat for 'lizard' on page 11 and 'salamander' on page 14.
- Ask them to write out the words and, using reference, draw a picture to illustrate each word.

**Assessment** *(R, AF1)* Were children able to recognise and say the letters?

## Speaking, listening and drama activities

**Objective** Enjoy listening to and using spoken and written language and readily turn to it in play and learning (1.1).

- Play the memory game, 'I walked in the park and I found a...'
- Explain that each child must listen to the child before, then add a new word, e.g. 'I walked in the park and I found a leaf', 'I walked in the wood and I found a leaf and a frog'.
- When someone forgets one of the contributions, the game starts from the beginning again.

## Writing activities

**Objective** Attempt writing for various purposes, using features of different forms such as lists, stories (9.1).

- Discuss where the family took the salamander.
- Ask the children to suggest what sorts of animals might need rescuing and why. Write a list of ideas on the board.
- Talk about how important it is to look after animals, e.g. give them food, water and shelter.
- Ask the children to choose an animal that might need rescuing, draw and name it and then write a list of the things it needs.
- Make a display of the children's work headed 'Animal Rescue'.

**Assessment** *(W, AF3)* Were children able to order their thoughts in a list?

# The Lost Puppy

| | |
|---|---|
| **C** = Language comprehension | *R, AF* = QCA reading assessment focus |
| **W** = Word recognition | *W, AF* = QCA writing assessment focus |

## Group or guided reading

### Introducing the book

**C** *(Prediction)* Look at the cover and read the title. Ask the children: *What do you think will happen in this story?*

**C** *(Clarifying)* Look through the book at the illustrations and confirm the children's predictions.

**W** Point to the word 'couldn't' on page 7 and tell the children the word.

### Strategy check

Remind the children to read from left to right.

### Independent reading

- Ask children to read the story. Praise and encourage them while they read, and prompt as necessary.

**W** Praise the children for reading the high frequency words and CVC words on sight.

**W** Encourage children to work out the decodable words by sounding out and blending the phonemes all through the word. Help children read the tricky words: 'called', 'looked', 'couldn't', 'find', 'everyone', 'nobody' and 'bone'.

**Assessment** Check that children:

- *(R, AF1)* can read the high frequency words with confidence
- *(R, AF4)* track the text from left to right, top to bottom.

## Returning to the text

C *(Summarising)* Ask the children to retell the story in one or two sentences.

C *(Clarifying, Questioning)* Ask: *Do you think Floppy was a clever dog? What was Floppy really looking for?*

W Ask: *What was the name of the puppy? Find the word in the story. Find another word with a double 'f' at the end.* ('off' page 2)

C *(Imagining)* Talk about what Mrs May and the children might have been calling when they were looking for Sniff. Ask: *What is Floppy doing?* (sniffing!)

W Look at page 7. Point out the words 'find' and 'Sniff'. Point out how the grapheme 'i' has a different sound in each of the words.

# Group and independent reading activities

**Objective** Use talk to organise, sequence and clarify thinking (3.2). Retell narratives in the correct sequence, drawing on the language patterns of stories (7.4).

C *(Summarising)* In pairs, ask the children to retell the story to their partners without looking at the storybook.

- To check, ask them to reread the story to make sure they didn't leave anything out.
- Did any children remember the order that the characters looking for the puppy were mentioned: Biff and Chip, Wilf and Wilma, Mum and Dad?

**Assessment** *(R, AF2)* Did the children memorise some of the phrases in the story?

**Objective** Know that print carries meaning and, in English, is read from left to right (7.1).

C *(Clarifying)* Write the following jumbled sentences on the board:

a puppy had Mrs May
was lost Sniff
Sniff find They couldn't
by tree the Sniff was

- Ask the children to rearrange the words to make sensible sentences, writing the sentences out.
- They can use the book to check.

**Assessment** *(R, AF3)* Do they recognise that capital letters start sentences?

**Objective** Hear and say sounds in words in the order in which they occur (5.5).

**W** Ask the children to find the word 'dog' in the story.

- Invite children to say the three sounds in the word and to write the word on the board.
- Ask children, in pairs, to find other CVC words, e.g. 'had', 'ran', 'his', 'for'. These are all decodable words, whilst 'was' is a tricky word.
- In turn, one child reads the word, sounding out the letters, the other listens to each sound and writes down the word.
- Children check their words by looking in the book.

**Assessment** *(R, AF1)* Can children hear the letter sounds in each word?

## Speaking, listening and drama activities

**Objective** Use language to imagine and recreate roles and experiences (1.3, 4.1).

- Arrange the children in a circle and pass a toy dog or other soft toy to a child. Ask the child to say one word to describe how he/she thinks Mrs May feels at losing her puppy.
- After saying a word, e.g. 'worried', the child passes the toy around the circle.
- Record the children's suggestions on a flip chart or board.

- Talk about times when you have lost something and what you did to find it.
- Ask children to talk about things they have lost and how they felt about it.
- Invite children to describe their feelings when the thing they lost was found.

## Writing activities

**Objective** Attempt writing for various purposes, using features of different forms (9.1).

- Explain that sometimes when someone loses something they put up a notice describing the thing they have lost, e.g. a missing cat.
- Talk about the kinds of things that would be useful to include on a poster for a missing dog, e.g. size, colour, name, contact telephone number, picture of the dog, etc.
- Ask the children to design and write a poster that Mrs May might have written if Sniff hadn't been found.
- Together, think of ideas and write on the board for the children to glean from.

**Assessment** *(W, AF3)* Were children able to include useful information in their poster?

# New Trees

C = Language comprehension  *R, AF* = QCA reading assessment focus
W = Word recognition  *W, AF* = QCA writing assessment focus

## Group or guided reading

### Introducing the book

C *(Prediction)* Show the cover to the children. Read the title and the poster. Ask: *What do you think will happen in this story?*

C *(Clarifying)* Ask: *What does it mean when it says trees will help the park?* Talk about how trees are good for the environment, they provide homes and food for animals, they look nice, they are fun to play in, etc.

W Point to the word 'stream' on page 7 and tell the children the word.

### Strategy check

Remind the children to read from left to right.

### Independent reading

- Ask children to read the story. Praise and encourage them while they read, and prompt as necessary.

W Praise the children for reading the high frequency words and CVC words on sight.

W Encourage children to work out the decodable words by sounding out and blending the phonemes all through the word.

**Assessment** Check that children:

- *(R, AF1)* use the context to help them read unfamiliar words.
- *(R, AF1)* can read on sight the familiar high frequency words
- *(R, AF1)* recognise words from previous stories.

- Following on from what the children have learned about different trees, invite children to tell the rest of the class something about a chosen tree, e.g. the shape and colour of its leaves, where it grows, how big it grows, etc. Encourage them to use props and pictures to enhance their presentation.

## Writing activities

**Objective** Write their own names and other things such as labels (11.1).

- Ask children to draw a tree of their choice.
- Make a class display entitled 'park' or 'wood'.
- Stick the trees onto the display and ask each child to write a label that can be attached to the tree they have drawn. The label should say something like, 'Oak tree planted by Ella'.
- Allow the children to decide where they would like their tree to be positioned on the display.

**Assessment** *(W, AF2)* Did the children start to use some punctuation?

# Up and Down

C = Language comprehension    *R, AF* = QCA reading assessment focus

W = Word recognition    *W, AF* = QCA writing assessment focus

## Group or guided reading

### Introducing the book

C *(Clarifying)* Look at the cover and read the title. Discuss what the 'shop guide' says. Ask: *What is 'hardware'?*

C *(Clarifying)* Ask: *Do you know what the special staircase is called in the picture?*

C *(Prediction)* Ask the children to say what they think the story is about.

C *(Clarifying)* Look through the book together to confirm their predictions.

### Strategy check

Remind the children to use their phonic knowledge to work out new words.

### Independent reading

- Ask children to read the story. Praise and encourage them while they read, and prompt as necessary.

W Praise the children for reading the high frequency words and CVC words on sight.

W Point out the word 'paintbrush' and ask the children which two words make up the whole word.

**Assessment** Check that children:

- *(R, AF2)* notice and attempt to read the signs and notices in the illustration to help them understand where the characters are
- *(R, AF1)* read high frequency words confidently.

## Returning to the text

C *(Summarising)* Ask the children to retell the story in one or two sentences.

C *(Questioning)* Ask: *Do you think Mum is going to want to go shopping with Dad again?*

C *(Clarifying)* Ask: *Has anyone been on an escalator? Tell me some good things about escalators and some not so good things* (good – you don't need to walk upstairs, etc.; bad – you can't change your mind and walk down an escalator that is going up, etc.).

W Turn to pages 2–3 and look at some of the shop signs. Write the words on the board. Ask: *What two words make up 'outfits'?* Tell the children the words 'fashions' and 'hosiery'. Ask: *What do you think 'hosiery' means?*

# Group and independent reading activities

**Objective** Use talk to organise, sequence and clarify thinking (3.2). Show an understanding of the elements of stories, such as main character, sequence of events (7.3).

C *(Summarising)* Ask the children the following questions to establish the correct sequence of events:

*Where did Mum and Dad go?*
*Why did Mum go down a level?*
*What happened next?*
*Turn to pages 8 and 9. Why didn't Mum stop on the second level?*
*Why did Dad go up?*
*How did Mum and Dad finally get to meet on the same floor?*

- Ask: *How many times did Dad go to the third level? How many times did Mum? Did Dad ever go to the first level?*

**Assessment** *(R, AF2)* Do children remember the sequence of events?

**Objective** Know that print carries meaning and, in English, is read from left to right (7.1).

**C** *(Clarifying)* Write each word from the following sentences on individual word cards:

Mum and Dad went shopping.
Dad wanted a book.
Mum wanted a paintbrush.
Dad went up.
Mum couldn't see Dad.

- Give each pair of children jumbled word cards for one sentence. Ask them to rearrange the cards to make the sentence.
- Children continue to make all the sentences by swapping their cards with another pair of children.
- Finally, jumble all the cards and ask the children to make as many sentences as they can.

**Assessment** *(R, AF2)* Do children reread the sentences to check for sense?

**Objective** Read some high frequency words (5.9).

**W** Prepare word cards with the words 'up' and 'down'.

- Say an action and hold up either the 'up' or 'down' card for the children to follow, e.g. say 'jump' and hold up the 'up' card and children read the word and jump up.
- Repeat with other actions, e.g. look, bend, arms up, etc.
- Prepare more 'up' and 'down' word cards and give to a group.
- Ask the other children to stand up or crouch down, for example, and the group with the word cards holds up the correct word.

**Assessment** *(R, AF1)* Were children able to read and understand the word?

## Speaking, listening and drama activities

**Objective** Use language to imagine and recreate roles (4.1, 8.3).

- In pairs, ask the children to take the roles of Mum and Dad.
- Ask them to act out the play by imagining what Mum and Dad say to each other on each page, e.g.

page 1 Mum: I am going to buy a brush.
Dad: I am going to buy a book.
Page 2 Mum: Bye, see you in a minute.

## Writing activities

**Objective** Attempt writing for various purposes, using features of different forms such as lists (9.1).

- Create a shop corner in the classroom, if there isn't already one.
- Ask the children to suggest what items could be bought in the shop, perhaps using some of the items mentioned in the book. Write the words on the board.
- Ask the children to draw pictures of the items mentioned and then place them in the shop corner.
- Ask the children to write a shopping list of four items they would like to buy from the shop using the words on the board.
- Taking it in turns, ask small groups of children to go to the shop corner and purchase the items on their list.

**Assessment** *(W, AF2)* Were children able to match the word with the picture?

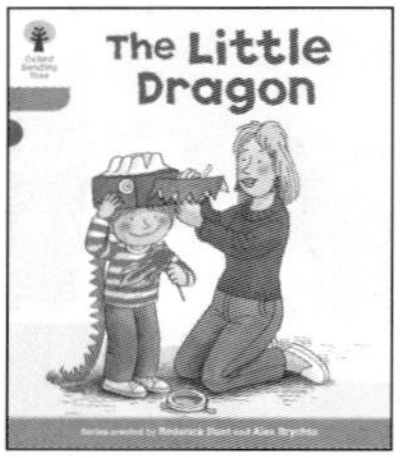


# The Little Dragon

**C** = Language comprehension  *R, AF* = QCA reading assessment focus
**W** = Word recognition  *W, AF* = QCA writing assessment focus

## Group or guided reading

### Introducing the book

**C** *(Prediction)* Look at the cover. Read the title and ask the children to predict what the story is about.

**C** *(Clarifying)* Look through the book at the illustrations and confirm the children's predictions.

**W** Ask the children to say if they recognise any of the characters, e.g. Dad, Wilf, etc. Point out the words 'king', 'knight', 'princess' and 'dragon' and ask: *Who is playing the part of the king?*

### Strategy check

Remind the children to segment new words into sounds to work them out.

### Independent reading

- Ask children to read the story. Praise and encourage them while they read, and prompt as necessary.

**W** Encourage children to work out the decodable words by sounding out and blending the phonemes all through the word. Help children read the tricky words ('knight', 'fight' and 'frightened'), pointing out the 'igh' sound in each of the words.

**Assessment** Check that children:

- *(R, AF1)* use a range of strategies to work out new words
- read the speech with appropriate expression.

## Returning to the text

**C** *(Clarifying, Questioning)* Ask: *Do you think Dad enjoyed being a tree? Why are his arms sticking out? Why aren't they sticking out at the end of the play? Try holding your arms out for a long time.*

**W** On page 1 ask the children to find the word on the sign that Wilf is holding up. Say the word and explain that a play is divided up into scenes.

**C** *(Clarifying)* Ask: *How many scenes are in this play? What happened to Wilf's sign on page 7?*

**C** *(Imagining)* Find out from the children which character they would like to play and why.

**W** Ask the children to find words with 'ss' at the end of them ('cross', 'princess'). Ask: *What does the 's' on the end of 'dragons' tell us?*

**C** *(Clarifying)* On page 15, ask: *Why did Wilf throw confetti on Wilma? Do you think Wilma knew she was going to be pushed in the pond?*

# Group and independent reading activities

**Objective** Use language to imagine and recreate roles and experiences (4, 8.3).

**C** *(Summarising)* In pairs, ask the children to choose a scene from the play and retell that part of the story through the eyes of Dad.

- Encourage the children to use the illustrations to add extra detail to the story, e.g. 'I was so surprised when Wilma rushed on and shouted I dropped my leaves'.

**Assessment** *(R, AF2)* Do children empathise with Dad's role in the play?

**Objective** Know that print carries meaning and, in English, is read from left to right (7.1).

**C** *(Clarifying)* Write the following jumbled sentences on the board:

"I Chip am," said the king.

"knight I am the," said Wilma.
"Kipper am I," said the dragon.
"good What a play," everyone said.

- Ask the children to rearrange the words to make sensible sentences, writing them out and using the book to check.

**Assessment** *(R, AF3)* Do they recognise that capital letters start sentences?

**Objective** Use phonic knowledge to write simple regular words and make phonetically plausible attempts at more complex words (5.10, 6.1).

- (W) Turn to page 11 and ask the children to tell you where Biff and Kipper played (under the tree).
- Turn to page 15 and ask: *Where did Biff push Wilma?* (in the pond)
- Talk about the other preposition on page 1 (on).
- Give pairs of children word cards 'in', 'on' and 'under'.
- Using props such as a box and a book, ask the children to hold up the correct word to describe where you have positioned the book in relation to the box.

**Assessment** *(R, AF1)* Do children show you the correct word?

## Speaking, listening and drama activities

**Objective** Use language to imagine and recreate roles and experiences (1.3, 4.1).

- Ask the children, in groups of six, to act out the whole play.
- Explain that there are six parts: king, dragon, tree, princess, knight and Wilf.
- Support children in deciding who should play which part, discussing the important 'backstage' part that Wilf plays.
- Encourage children to learn their lines, speaking them with the appropriate intonation and expression. The words could also be written on the board.

- Children who aren't immediately performing a part could add sound effects, e.g. splashing water on page 15.
- Once children feel confident with their production, invite groups to perform their play to the others.

## Writing activities

**Objective** Attempt writing for various purposes, using features of different forms such as lists (9.1).

- Discuss the parts played by the story characters.
- Model how to write the title of the play and the cast list.
- Ask the children to design a poster to advertise the play. The poster must include the title of the play plus a cast list. (The cast list could be taken from the story or the cast list based on the group play performed in the Speaking and listening activity.)

  **The Little Dragon**

  | | |
  |---|---|
  | The tree | Dad |
  | The king | Chip |
  | Etc. | |

- To complete the poster, ask the children to draw a picture depicting one scene from the play.
- Remind the children of the purpose of a poster – to attract people to see the play.

**Assessment** *(W, AF2)* Does the poster include all relevant information?

# The Band

| | |
|---|---|
| C = Language comprehension | *R, AF* = QCA reading assessment focus |
| W = Word recognition | *W, AF* = QCA writing assessment focus |

## Group or guided reading

### Introducing the book

C Look at the cover and discuss what is happening in the picture. Do the children recognise anyone?

C *(Clarifying)* Read the title. Talk about what a band is. Ask: *Do you know of anyone who plays in a band or orchestra?*

C *(Prediction)* Look together at page 1 and ask the children to predict what will happen in the story.

### Strategy check

Remind the children to use their knowledge of phonics to work out new words.

### Independent reading

- Ask children to read the story. Praise and encourage them while they read, and prompt as necessary.

W Praise the children for reading the high frequency words and CVC words on sight.

W Encourage children to work out the decodable words by sounding out and blending the phonemes all through the word, e.g. ('t–r–u–m–p–e–t'). Help children with the tricky words, e.g. 'garage' ('g–a–r–a–ge') and 'couldn't' ('c–oul–d–nt').

**Assessment** Check that children:

- *(R, AF1)* can read the high frequency words with confidence
- *(R, AF4)* track the text from left to right, top to bottom.

## Returning to the text

C *(Summarising)* Ask the children to retell the story in one or two sentences.

C *(Clarifying, Questioning)* Ask: *Why did Floppy always bark when Dad played his trumpet? Do you think Dad will be asked to play in the band again? Do you think Floppy was really bad?*

W Ask the children to list all the places that Dad played his trumpet, writing them out as a list: 'house', 'garage', 'shed', 'park'.

C *(Questioning)* Ask: *Why is the band playing in the park? Who might listen to the band? Show me the bandstand.*

# Group and independent reading activities

**Objective** Use talk to organise, sequence and clarify thinking (3.2). Show an understanding of the elements of stories, such as main character, sequence of events (7.3).

C *(Questioning)* Invite one child to be Dad.

- Give children word cards with either 'what', 'why' or 'where' written on them.
- Encourage children to ask a question according to the word written on their card, e.g. 'What instrument did you play?'
- 'Dad' answers the question.
- When 'Dad' has answered four or five questions, invite a child to be Floppy.
- Children ask Floppy four or five questions.
- Repeat with a child being Mum.

**Assessment** *(R, AF2)* Did the children choose questions based on the plot and setting. Did the children need to refer to the story before forming their questions?

**Objective** Know that print carries meaning and, in English, is read from left to right (7.1).

**W** Prepare photocopied sheets of the following unfinished sentences:

Dad played ________ the shed.
Floppy barked at ________.
Floppy ________ to the park.
The band couldn't ________.
"What ________ bad dog!"

- Give out the sheets to the children and ask them to read the sentences and to guess what word would make sense in the gaps.
- Ask the children to fill in the missing words and then check their sentences with those in the book.

**Assessment** *(R, AF2)* Do children reread their sentences to check for sense?

**Objective** Explore and experiment with sounds, words and texts (5.1).

**W** Ask the children to find the word 'play' in the story.

- Encourage them to then find another word that has 'play' in it. Ask: *What letters have been added to 'play' to make another word? ('-ed') Find me other words in the story that end in '-ed'.*
- Write a list on the board. Ask: *What is the word without the '–ed' on the end or the root word?*
- Give the children copies of 'The Little Dragon' and 'The Lost Puppy' and ask them to find more '-ed' words.
- With the children, prepare a poster of '-ed' words with the root word that children can add to.

**Assessment** *(R, AF1)* Do children recognise the root words inside the '-ed' words?

## Speaking, listening and drama activities

**Objective** Sustain attentive listening, responding to what they have heard by relevant comments, questions or actions (2.2).

- Look together at the illustration on pages 8 and 9. Talk about the instruments and discuss their names. (left to right: 'drum', 'clarinet', 'trumpet', 'trombone' and 'tuba')
- Explain that the drum is a percussion instrument, the clarinet a wind instrument and the last three, brass instruments.
- Gather together as many musical instruments as possible, plus books or posters about musical instruments.
- Invite children to make a sound on one of the instruments, one at a time. Ask them if they know the name of the instrument and whether it fits into any of the instrument categories discussed earlier.
- Make a table with the following category headings: 'percussion', 'wind', 'brass' and 'string'. With the help of the children fill in the table.
- Once they are familiar with the instruments, invite children in turn to mime playing an instrument of their choice. The other children guess what the instrument is.

## Writing activities

**Objective** Write their own names and other things such as labels and captions (11.1).

- Ask the children to choose a favourite instrument and to draw and label it.
- Collect the drawings together and make a class book about musical instruments.

**Assessment** *(W, AF3)* Were children able to label their drawing correctly?

**INSPIRATIONAL SUPPORT FOR TEACHERS**
For free professional development videos from leading experts, plus other resources and free eBooks, please go to **www.oxfordprimary.co.uk**

**HELPING YOU ENGAGE PARENTS**
We have researched the most common concerns and worries parents have about their children's literacy and provide answers and support in **www.oxfordowl.co.uk**

This site contains advice on how to share a book, how to pronounce pure sounds, how to encourage boys' reading, and much more. We hope you will find the site useful and recommend it to your parents.

OXFORD
UNIVERSITY PRESS

Great Clarendon Street, Oxford OX2 6DP

Oxford University Press is a department of the University of Oxford. It furthers the University's objective of excellence in research, scholarship, and education by publishing worldwide in

Oxford New York
Auckland Cape Town Dar es Salaam Hong Kong Karachi
Kuala Lumpur Madrid Melbourne Mexico City Nairobi
New Delhi Shanghai Taipei Toronto

With offices in

Argentina Austria Brazil Chile Czech Republic France
Greece Guatemala Hungary Italy Japan Poland
Portugal Singapore South Korea Switzerland
Thailand Turkey Ukraine Vietnam



Written by Lucy Tritton, based on the original characters created by Roderick Hunt and Alex Brychta.



First published 2008
This edition published 2011



British Library Cataloguing in Publication Data

Data available

Cover illustrations Alex Brychta

ISBN: 978-0-19-848168-3

10 9 8 7 6 5 4 3 2

Page make-up by Thomson Digital

Printed in China by Imago

Paper used in the production of this book is a natural, recyclable product made from wood grown in sustainable forests. The manufacturing process conforms to the environmental regulations of the country of origin.